Continents

A Bulletin Board in a Book!

Sunflower
education

Exceptional Books for Teachers and Parents

Editorial
Sunflower Education

Design
Cynthia Hannon Design

Illustrations:
Cover and interior images: © Shutterstock Images LLC

ISBN-13: 978-1-937166-14-4
ISBN-10: 1-937166-14-7

Table of Contents

To the Teacher

Activity Sheets
The Continents
Asia
Africa
North America
South America
Antarctica
Europe
Australia

Posters
Continents
Continent Facts
Asia
Asia Map
Africa
Africa Map
North America
North America Map
South America
South America Map
Antarctica
Antarctica Map
Europe
Europe Map
Australia
Australia Map
Remember the Continents!

To the Teacher

Continents: A Bulletin Board in a Book! consists of two main parts: bulletin-board posters and student activity sheets. They are designed to be used together.

There are 17 posters:
- 1—Continents (title poster **A**)
- 1—Continents Facts (subtitle poster **B**)
- 7—Continent Facts Posters
- 7—Continent Map Posters
- 1—Remember the Continents! Poster (**C**)

There are 8 student activity sheets:
- 1—on continents in general
- 7—continent-specific

Place posters to show relative locations of continents.

❶ **Post the Bulletin-Board Display**
- Copy the posters or cut them out.
- See the illustration for suggested layout.
- Post the Continents (title poster) and Continents Facts (subtitle poster) posters together to form the top or central part of the display.
- Pair each Continent Facts Poster with its corresponding Continent Map Poster.
- Post the Remember the Continents! Poster in a prominent place.

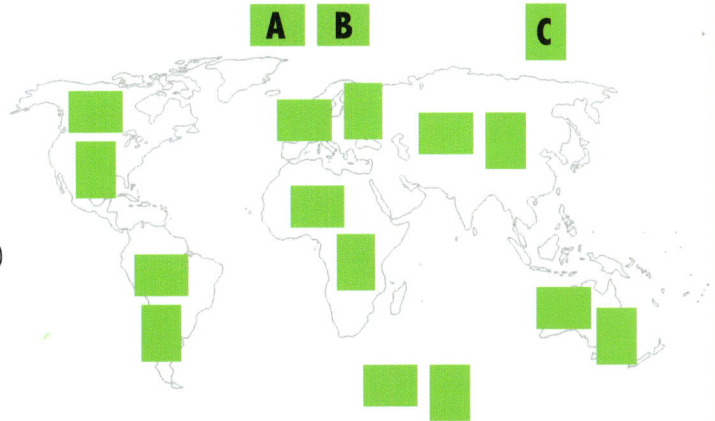

❷ **Discuss Continents with Students**
- Lead a discussion about the continents. Allow students time to peruse the posters. Ensure students understand the concepts of area, longest distances, population, and countries.
- Encourage students to memorize the names and sizes of the continents. Work with students to complete the Remember the Continents! Poster. Explain that the letters are the first letter of each continent's name and that the letters represent the continents from largest to smallest. Encourage students to come up with a memorable phrase (for example, "An Ape Needs Some Apple Eating Ants") as a mnemonic device.
- Focus students' attention on the small locator maps on the Continent Facts Posters (point out the red indicator arrows) and the larger Continent Map Posters. Encourage them to memorize the shapes and locations of the continents.

❸ **Share the Activity sheets**
- All of the activity sheets can be completed using information from the posters. Consider having students complete the activity sheets either as assessment or with access to the bulletin board.
- Students can complete the activity sheets individually or with partners.

Emphasize the vast sizes of the continents, the great distances across them, and, except for Antarctica, their huge populations. Have fun sharing the world with your students!

Worksheet Answers

The Continents
1. 1. North America;
2. South America; 3. Europe;
4. Africa; 5. Asia; 6. Australia;
7. Antarctica.
2. 2, 5, 1, 7, 6, 3, 4
3. Reward earnest answers.
4. Verify correct answers.
5. Reward earnest answers.

Asia
1. X should be on Asia.
2. 6,000 miles
3. Three Asian countries should be listed.
4. 4 billion
5. Europe and Africa

Africa
1. X should be on Africa.
2. 5,000 miles
3. Three African countries should be listed.
4. 1 billion
5. Asia

North America
1. X should be on North America.
2. 4,500 miles
3. Three North American countries should be listed.
4. 530 million
5. South America

South America
1. X should be on South America.
2. 4,800 miles
3. Three South American countries should be listed.
4. 400 million
5. North America

Antarctica
1. X should be on Antarctica.
2. 3,500 miles
3. Many countries
4. Answers may vary slightly. A few people; 3,000 scientists.
5. No

Europe
1. X should be on Europe.
2. 4,000 miles
3. Three European countries should be listed.
4. 700 million
5. Asia

Australia
1. X should be on Australia.
2. 2,800 miles
3. Australia
4. 21 million
5. No

The Continents

1 Write the name of each continent by the correct number below.

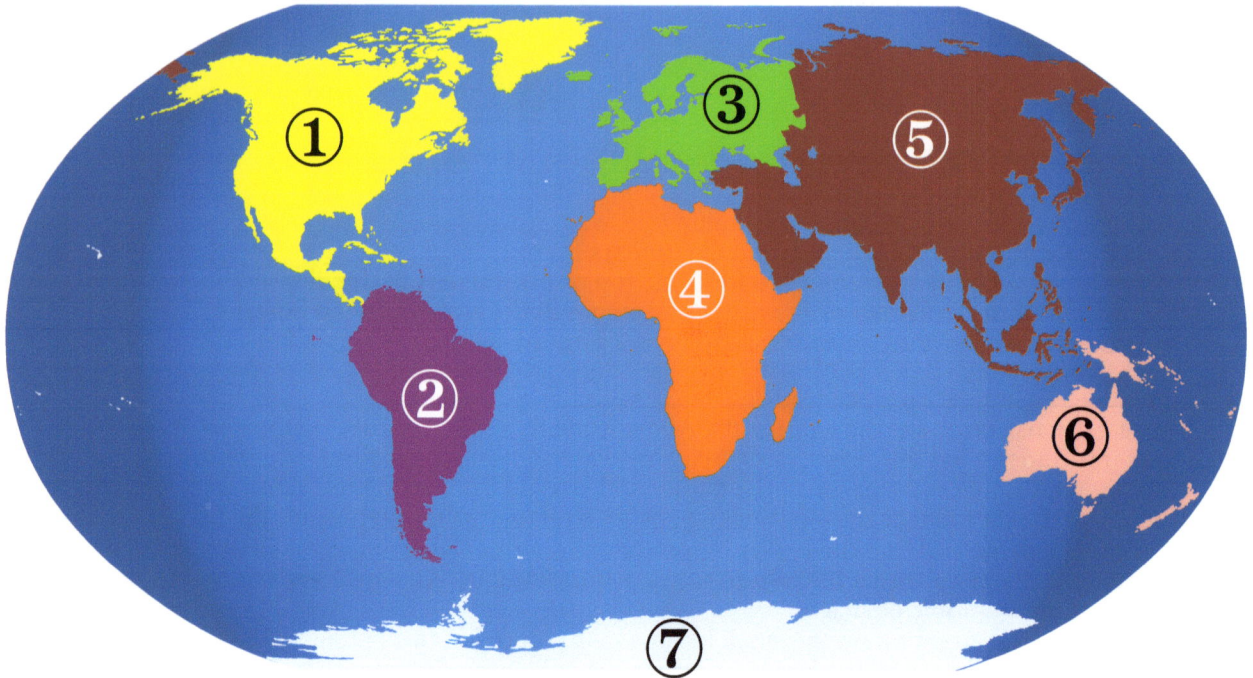

① _____

② _____

③ _____

④ _____

⑤ _____

⑥ _____

⑦ _____

2 Number the continents from 1 to 7. Write 1 next to the biggest continent. Write 2 next to the second-biggest continent. Keep going until you number all 7.

____ Africa ____ Europe

____ Antarctica ____ North America

____ Asia ____ South America

____ Australia

3 Write something you think is interesting about the continents.

———————————————————————————————————————

———————————————————————————————————————

———————————————————————————————————————

4 Which continent do you live on?

———————————————————————————————————————

5 Would you like to visit another continent? Why?

———————————————————————————————————————

———————————————————————————————————————

———————————————————————————————————————

Asia

1 Where is Asia? Put an X on the map to show where Asia is.

2 What is the greatest distance in Asia?

_____

3 What are two countries in Asia?

_____

_____

4 How many people live in Asia?

_____

5 Which continents border Asia?

_____

_____

Africa

1 Where is Africa? Put an X on the map to show where Africa is.

2 What is the greatest distance in Africa?

_____

3 What are two countries in Africa?

_____

_____

4 How many people live in Africa?

_____

5 Which continent borders Africa?

_____

_____

North America

1 Where is North America? Put an X on the map to show where North America is.

2 What is the greatest distance in North America?

_____

3 What are two countries in North America?

_____

_____

4 How many people live in North America?

_____

5 Which continent borders North America?

_____

_____

South America

1 Where is South America? Put an X on the map to show where South America is.

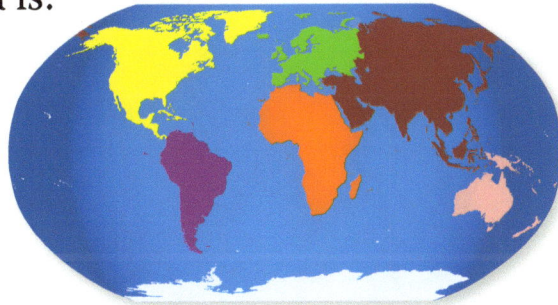

2 What is the greatest distance in South America?

_____

3 What are two countries in South America?

_____

_____

4 How many people live in South America?

_____

5 Which continent borders South America?

_____

_____

Antarctica

1 Where is Antarctica? Put an X on the map to show where Antarctica is.

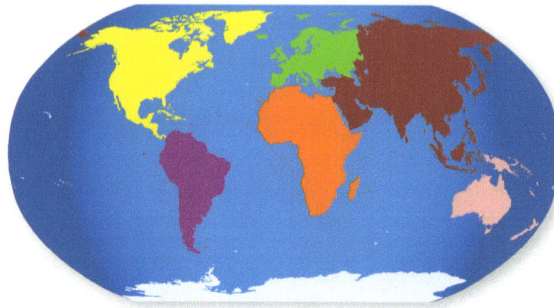

2 What is the greatest distance in Antarctica?

_____

3 Who controls Antarctica?

_____

_____

4 How many people live in Antarctica?

_____

_____

5 Do any continents border Antarctica?

_____

Europe

1 Where is Europe? Put an X on the map to show where Europe is.

2 What is the greatest distance in Europe?

_____

3 What are two countries in Europe?

_____

_____

4 How many people live in Europe?

_____

5 Which continent borders Europe?

_____

_____

Australia

1 Where is Australia? Put an X on the map to show where Australia is.

2 What is the greatest distance in Australia?

_____

3 What country is in Australia?

_____

_____

4 How many people live in Australia?

_____

5 Do any continents border Australia?

_____

_____

continents

The part of the Earth that is not covered by water is called *the land.*

The land is separated by oceans into seven huge pieces. The huge pieces of land are called *continents.* Each continent has its own name.

Asia • Africa • North America • South America • Europe • Antarctica • Australia

Continents Facts

How Many? There are seven continents.

How Big? Continents cover about one-third of the Earth! The biggest continent is Asia. The smallest one is Australia.

How Important? Continents form the land on which almost all people live. Plants and animals also live on the land. Rivers and lakes on the land give us water.

Did You Know? Some of the land is not part of any continent. These are the many islands in the Pacific Ocean. There are almost 30,000 of them! These islands are called Oceania. They range in size from very small to very large.

Asia

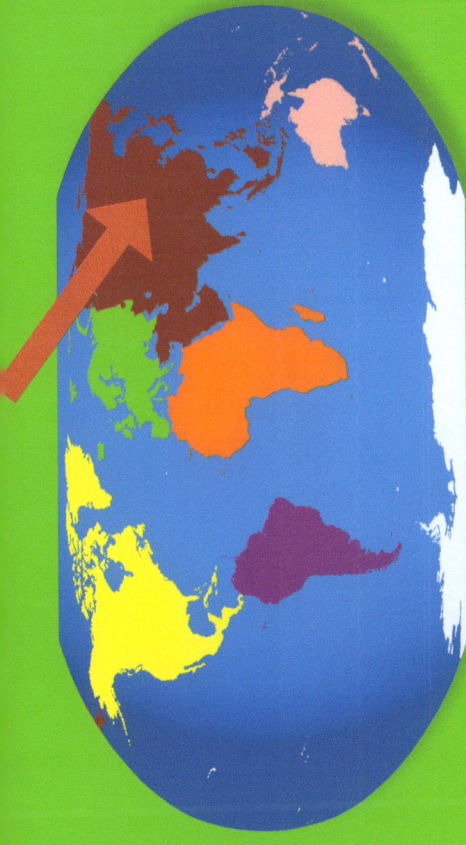

How Big?

Asia has an area of 17 million square miles. It is the biggest continent.

How Far?

Asia's longest distances are 6,000 miles east to west and 5,400 miles north to south.

Who's There?

About 4 billion people live in 50 countries in Asia.

Did You Know?

More than half of all the people in the world live in Asia.

Asia

Russia

Kazakhstan

Mongolia

Georgia

Kyrgyzstan

North Korea

Japan

Uzbekistan

Armenia
Turkey

Turkmenistan

Tajikistan

South Korea

Azerbaijan

China

Cyprus
Lebanon
Israel

Syria

Afghanistan

Iraq

Iran

Jordan

Pakistan

Nepal

Bhutan

Saudi Arabia

India

Burma

Laos

United Arab Emirates

Oman

Thailand

Vietnam

Philippines

Yemen

Cambodia

Sri Lanka

Malaysia

Maldives

Indonesia

East Timor

Africa

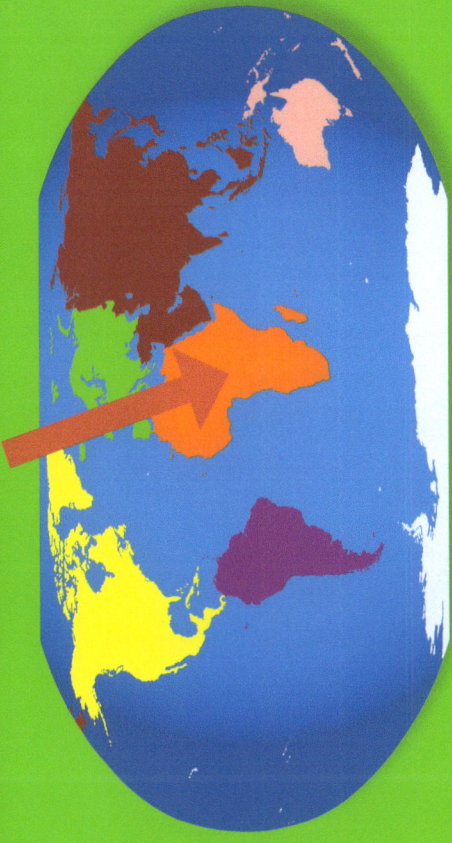

How Big?

Africa has an area of 12 million square miles. Africa is the second-biggest continent.

How Far?

Africa's longest distances are 5,000 miles north to south and 4,700 miles east to west.

Who's There?

About 1 billion people live in 53 countries in Africa.

Did You Know?

Africa is home to many famous animals. Monkeys, gorillas, giraffes, hippos, zebras, lions, and tigers all live in Africa.

Africa

Morocco · Tunisia · Algeria · Libya · Egypt · Western Sahara · Cape Verde · Mauritania · Mali · Niger · Chad · Sudan · Eritrea · Djibouti · Gambia · Senegal · Guinea · Burkina Faso · Benin · Nigeria · Guinea-Bissau · Côte d'Ivoire · Ghana · Togo · Sierra Leone · Liberia · Cameroon · Central African Republic · South Sudan · Ethiopia · Somalia · Equatorial Guinea · Sao Tome and Principe · Gabon · Congo · Democratic Republic of the Congo · Uganda · Kenya · Rwanda · Burundi · Tanzania · Angola · Comoros · Zambia · Malawi · Namibia · Zimbabwe · South Africa · Botswana · Mozambique · Madagascar · Lesotho · Swaziland

North America

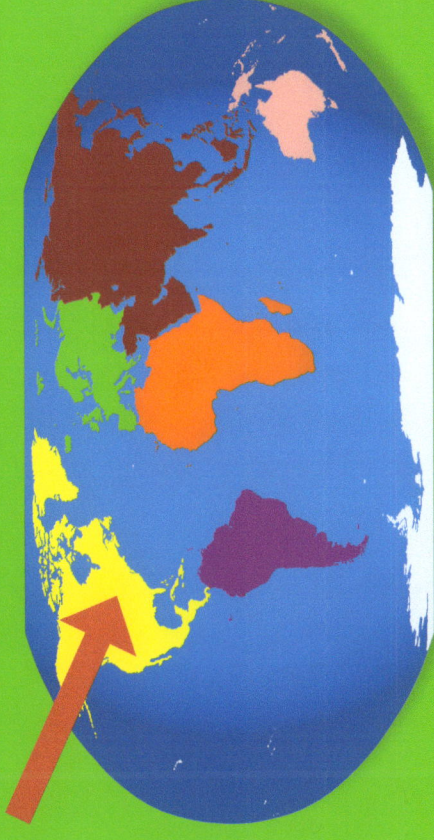

How Big?

North America has an area of 9.3 million square miles. North America is the third-biggest continent.

How Far?

North America's longest distances are 4,500 miles north to south and 4,000 miles east to west.

Who's There?

About 530 million people live in 23 countries in North America.

Did You Know?

The name "America" comes from an explorer. His name was Amerigo Vespucci. Over time, "Amerigo" became "America."

North America

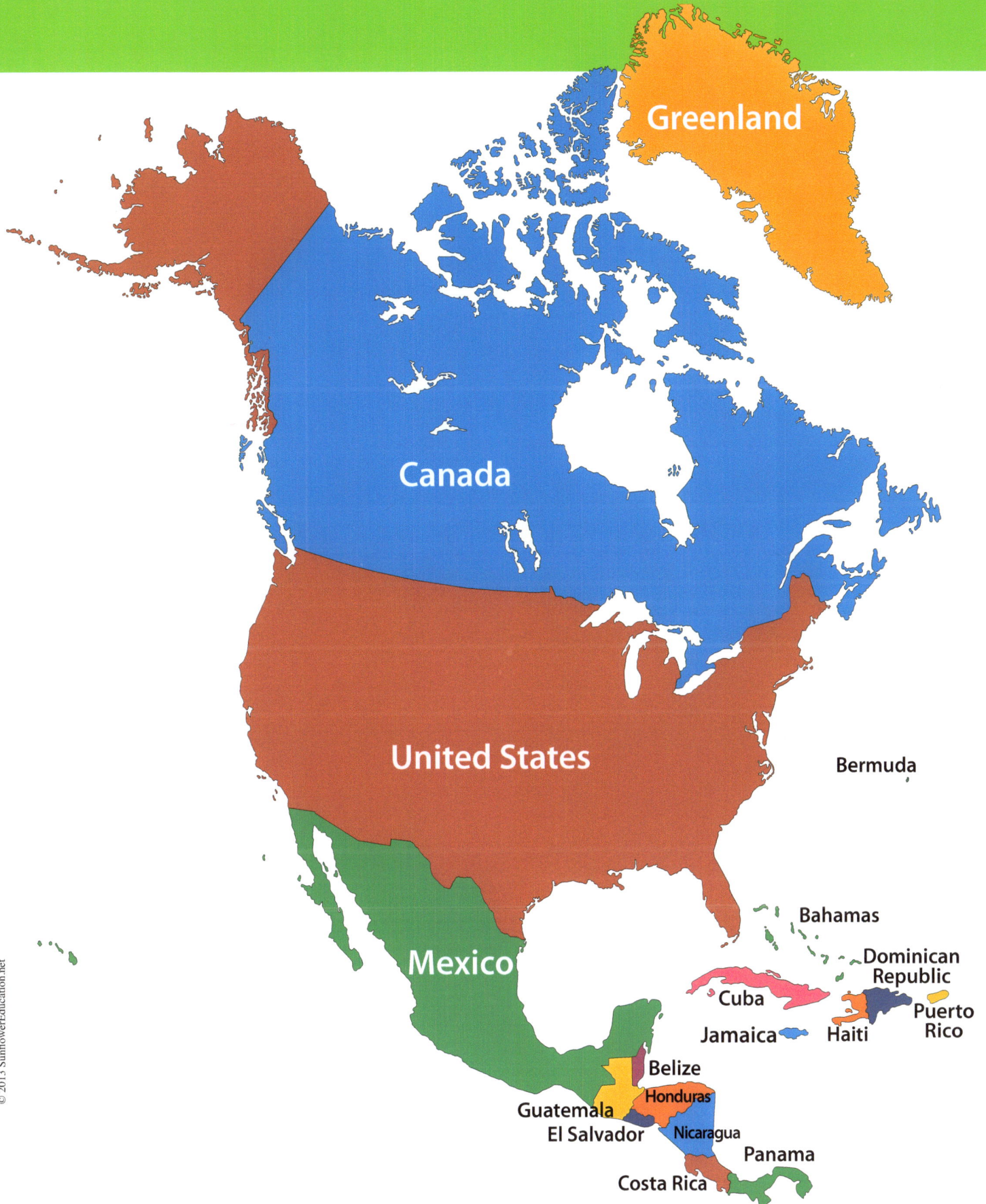

Greenland

Canada

United States

Bermuda

Mexico

Bahamas

Cuba

Dominican
Republic

Jamaica

Haiti

Puerto
Rico

Belize

Honduras

Guatemala

El Salvador

Nicaragua

Panama

Costa Rica

South America

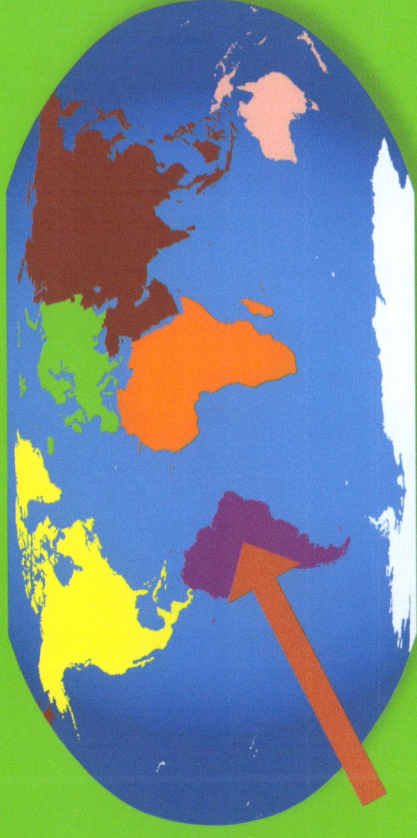

How Big?

South America has an area of 6.9 million square miles. South America is the fourth-biggest continent.

How Far?

South America's longest distances are 4,800 miles north to south and 3,200 miles east to west.

Who's There?

About 400 million people live in 12 countries in South America.

Did You Know?

Most people in South America speak Spanish. That is because people from Spain took over most of the continent long ago.

South America

Venezuela

Guyana

Suriname

French Guiana

Colombia

Ecuador

Peru

Brazil

Bolivia

Paraguay

Chile

Argentina

Uruguay

Falkland Islands

Antarctica

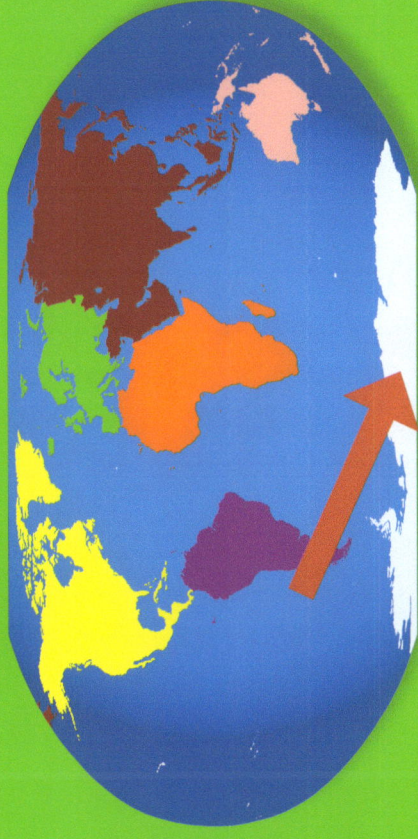

How Big?

Antarctica has an area of 4.7 million square miles. Antarctica is the fifth-biggest continent.

How Far?

Antarctica's longest distance is 3,500 miles across the continent.

Who's There?

It is very cold in Antarctica. Only a few people live there. At any time, about 3,000 scientists are in Antarctica doing research.

Did You Know?

Antarctica is the coldest, driest, and windiest continent. This is why few people live there.

Antarctica

Antarctica
(Controlled by many countries)

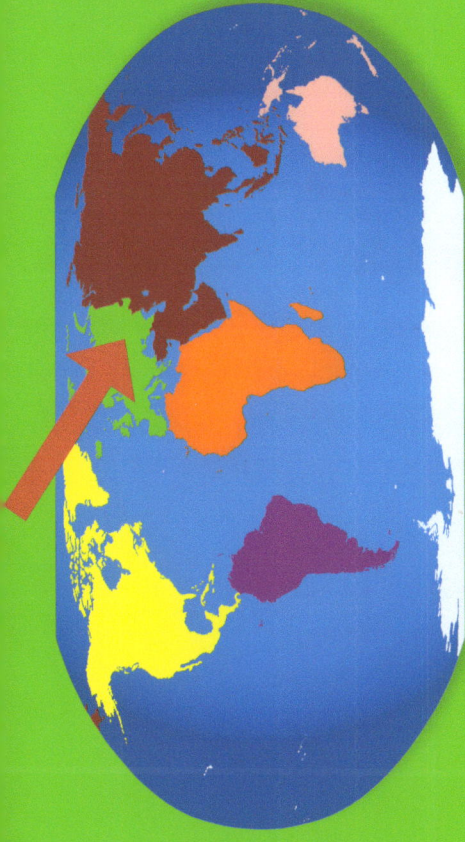

Europe

How Big?

Europe has an area of 4 million square miles. Europe is the sixth-biggest continent.

How Far?

Europe's longest distances are 4,000 miles east to west and 3,000 miles north to south.

Who's There?

About 700 million people live in 48 countries in Europe.

Did You Know?

Europe is one of the smallest continents in size. But it is one of the biggest in population.

Europe

Iceland

Sweden

Finland

Russia

Norway

Estonia

Latvia

Lithuania

Belarus

Denmark

Ireland

United Kingdom

Netherlands

Poland

Germany

Belgium

Ukraine

Luxembourg

Czech Republic

Slovakia

Moldova

Liechtenstein

Austria

Hungary

Romania

France

Switzerland

Slovenia

Croatia

Italy

Bosnia and Herzegovina

Serbia

Bulgaria

Montenegro

Portugal

Andorra

Macedonia

Albania

Spain

Greece

Australia

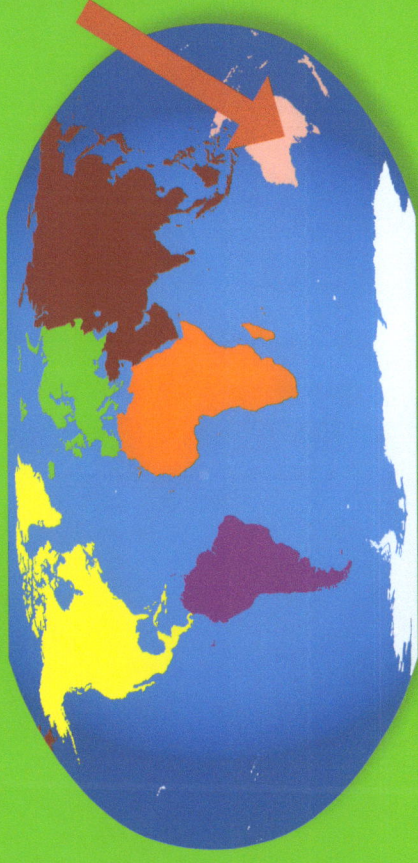

How Big?

Australia has an area of 3 million square miles. Australia is the smallest continent.

How Far?

Australia's longest distances are 2,500 miles east to west and 2,000 miles north to south.

Who's There?

About 21 million people live in one country in Australia.

Did You Know?

Australia is the only continent that has only one country. Both the country and the continent are called Australia.

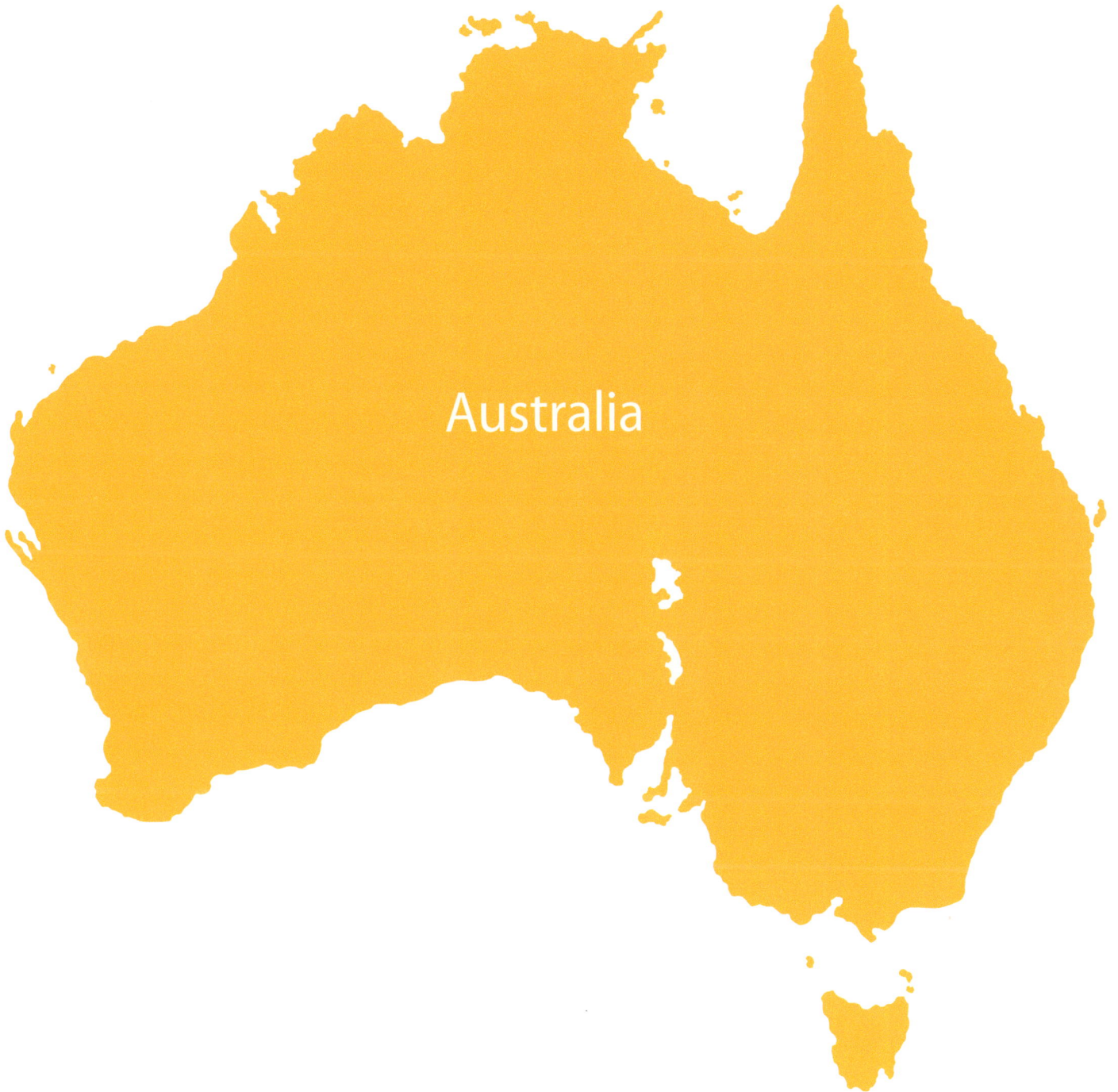

Australia

Australia

Remember the Continents!

A _____

A _____

N _____

S _____

A _____

E _____

A _____

www.ingramcontent.com/pod-product-compliance
Lightning Source LLC
Chambersburg PA
CBHW060832270326
41933CB00002B/61